Presented to

_____

by_____

on _____

Who Is Jesus?

Kathleen Long Bostrom
Illustrated by Elena Kucharik

TYNDALE KIDS

Tyndale House Publishers, Inc.
WHEATON, ILLINOIS

Library of Congress Cataloging-in-Publication Data

Bostrom, Kathleen Long.
        Who is Jesus? / Kathleen Long Bostrom; illustrated by Elena Kucharik.
            p.   cm. — (Questions from little hearts)
        Summary: A rhyming text consisting of questions to Jesus about what he was like, his
responses, and scriptural references to support the answers.
        ISBN 0-8423-5144-2 (hc)
        I. Jesus Christ—Biography—Juvenile literature. [I. Jesus Christ. 2. Bible—Selections.]
I. Kucharik, Elena, ill.   II. Title.   III. Series.
BT302.B587 1999
232—dc21   98-48044

Printed in Singapore

08   07   06   05
10   9   8

To my children, Christopher, Amy, and David,
Three of Christ's lights who show me God's love every day.
Love, Mom

Dear Jesus, please show me,

for I want to see

The ways you're the same

and yet different from me.

I'd like to know what

you were like as a boy.

Did you have a favorite
story or toy?

Did you take a short nap

when you needed to rest?

Were there special people

that you liked the best?

And what kinds of food

did you most like to eat?

I think I could live

on just ice cream and sweets!

What made you feel happy?

And what made you mad?

15

16

Was there ever a time

when you felt really sad?

Did you always take time

to pray every day?

When you talked to God,

tell me, what did you say?

20

I feel so unhappy

that you had to die.

Oh, why did that happen

to you, Jesus? Why?

I'M JESUS, GOD'S SON,

and I want you to see
The Bible can teach you
a lot about me.

I came from my Father
to show you the way
To live as God wants you
to live every day.

I came to the earth
    as a baby, like you,
So you have a birthday,
    and I have one too!

I came down from heaven
    as God's only Son
To show all the world
    that God loves everyone.

25

There isn't much written

   to help you to know

Just what I was like

   as a boy long ago.

I was, in some ways,

   just like all other kids.

I played, and I thought

   about things like they did.

The time hurried past,

    as I grew and I grew.

God loved me, and so did

    the people I knew.

I changed through the years

    from a boy to a man.

My life all along

    was a part of God's plan.

I loved to tell stories

to any who'd hear,

While people would gather

from far and from near.

They followed me closely

wherever I led,

So eager to hear

every word that I said.

I traveled a lot,

    walking mile after mile.

And when I got tired,

    I would sleep for a while.

One time when I just

    couldn't wait for a bed,

I curled up and slept

    in a rowboat instead.

I picked out twelve friends

who would travel with me

Wherever God sent me,

on land and on sea.

You, too, are my friends

if you do as I do

And love one another

as I have loved you.

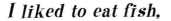

I liked to eat fish,

and I liked to eat bread.

I made sure that those

who were with me were fed.

So don't fret about

what you'll eat or you'll wear.

My Father will help you,

for he really cares.

43

I felt all the very same

feelings you feel.

The joy that I have

for my people is real.

I spoke out in anger

at people who lied;

47

I cried when I heard

that a good friend had died.

I prayed to my Father
in good times and bad.
He listened to every
concern that I had.

When you pray to God,
you should pray in my name,
For my love and God's love
are one and the same.

I died on a cross

so that others could live

And know there is nothing

that God can't forgive.

The day that I died

was a sad one, but then

God gave me a new life.

Now I live again!

I'm just like a lamp

glowing softly with light.

56

So you can feel safe

in the dark of the night.

But sometimes my love

is as bright as the sun

That shines like it has

since the world was begun.

So if you are willing,

please come, follow me.

Then you'll be my light

and will help people see

That God's love is so great,

it will never run out.

Now that is good news

to tell others about!

63

Bible References

Here are some Bible verses to talk about as you read this book again with your child. You may want to open your Bible as you read the verses. This will help your little one understand that Jesus' answers in this poem come from his Word, the Bible.

I'm Jesus, God's Son, and I want you to see
The Bible can teach you a lot about me.
I came from my Father to show you the way
To live as God wants you to live every day.

> I have given you an example to follow. JOHN 13:15

I came to the earth as a baby, like you,
So you have a birthday, and I have one too!
I came down from heaven as God's only Son
To show all the world that God loves everyone.

> So the baby born to you will be holy, and he will be called the Son of God. LUKE 1:35

> Christ, the Eternal Word: In the beginning the Word already existed. He was with God, and he was God. JOHN 1:1

There isn't much written to help you to know
Just what I was like as a boy long ago.
I was, in some ways, just like all other kids.
I played, and I thought about things like they did.

When Jesus was twelve years old, they attended the
[Passover] festival as usual. After the celebration was
over, they started home to Nazareth, but Jesus stayed
behind in Jerusalem. His parents didn't miss
him at first, because they assumed he
was with friends among the other
travelers. LUKE 2:42-44

The time hurried past,
    as I grew and I grew.
God loved me, and so did
    the people I knew.
I changed through the
    years from a boy to a man.
My life all along was a part of God's plan.

So Jesus grew both in height and in wisdom, and he was
loved by God and by all who knew him. LUKE 2:52

For God so loved the world that he gave his only Son.
JOHN 3:16

I loved to tell stories to any who'd hear,
While people would gather from far and from near.
They followed me closely wherever I led,
So eager to hear every word that I said.

> Jesus always used stories and illustrations like these when speaking to the crowds. MATTHEW 13:34

> Large crowds followed him wherever he went. MATTHEW 4:25

I traveled a lot, walking mile after mile.
And when I got tired, I would sleep for a while.
One time when I just couldn't wait for a bed,
I curled up and slept in a rowboat instead.

> One day Jesus said to his disciples, "Let's cross over to the other side of the lake." So they got into a boat and started out. On the way across, Jesus lay down for a nap, and while he was sleeping the wind began to rise. LUKE 8:22-23

I picked out twelve friends who would travel with me
Wherever God sent me, on land and on sea.
You, too, are my friends if you do as I do
And love one another as I have loved you.

Afterward Jesus went up on a mountain and called the ones he wanted to go with him. And they came to him. Then he selected twelve of them to be his regular companions, calling them apostles. . . . These are the names of the twelve he chose: Simon (he renamed him Peter), James and John (the sons of Zebedee, but Jesus nicknamed them "Sons of Thunder"), Andrew, Philip, Bartholomew, Matthew, Thomas, James (son of Alphaeus), Thaddaeus, Simon (the Zealot), Judas Iscariot (who later betrayed him). MARK 3:13-14; 16-19

I command you to love each other in the same way that I love you. . . . You are my friends if you obey me. JOHN 15:12, 14

I liked to eat fish, and I liked to eat bread.
I made sure that those who were with me were fed.
So don't fret about what you'll eat or you'll wear.
My Father will help you, for he really cares.

> Then Jesus took the loaves, gave thanks to God, and
> passed them out to the people. Afterward he did the
> same with the fish. And they all ate until they were full.
> JOHN 6:11

> So don't worry about having enough food or drink or
> clothing. . . . Your heavenly Father already knows all your
> needs, and he will give you all you need from day to day if
> you live for him and make the Kingdom of God your pri-
> mary concern. MATTHEW 6:31-33

I felt all the very same feelings you feel.
The joy that I have for my people is real.
I spoke out in anger at people who lied;
I cried when I heard that a good friend had died.

> I have told you this so that you will be filled with my joy.
> JOHN 15:11

> Then Jesus entered the Temple and began to drive out the
> merchants from their stalls. He told them, "The Scriptures
> declare, 'My Temple will be a place of prayer,' but you have
> turned it into a den of thieves." LUKE 19:45-46

When Jesus saw [Mary] weeping and saw the other people wailing with her, he was moved with indignation and was deeply troubled. "Where have you put him?" he asked them. They told him, "Lord, come and see." Then Jesus wept. JOHN 11:33-35

I prayed to my Father in good times and bad.
He listened to every concern that I had.
When you pray to God, you should pray in my name,
For my love and God's love are one and the same.

He went on a little farther and fell face down on the ground. He prayed that, if it were possible, the awful hour awaiting him might pass him by. MARK 14:35

The truth is, you can go directly to the Father and ask him, and he will grant your request because you use my name. You haven't done this before. Ask, using my name, and you will receive, and you will have abundant joy. JOHN 16:23-24

**I died on a cross so that others could live
And know there is nothing that God can't forgive.
The day that I died was a sad one, but then
God gave me a new life. Now I live again!**

Yes, it was written long ago that the Messiah must suffer and die and rise again from the dead on the third day. LUKE 24:46

I lay down my life voluntarily. For I have the right to lay it down when I want to and also the power to take it again. For my Father has given me this command. JOHN 10:18

God did not send his Son into the world to condemn it, but to save it. JOHN 3:17

**I'm just like a lamp glowing softly with light.
So you can feel safe in the dark of the night.
But sometimes my love is as bright as the sun
That shines like it has since the world was begun.**

Life itself was in him, and this life gives light to everyone. The light shines through the darkness, and the darkness can never extinguish it. JOHN 1:4-5

But while I am still here in the world, I am the light of the world. JOHN 9:5

So if you are willing, please come, follow me.
Then you'll be my light and will help people see
That God's love is so great, it will never run out.
Now that is good news to tell others about!

You are the light of the world—like a city on a mountain, glowing in the night for all to see. Don't hide your light under a basket! Instead, put it on a stand and let it shine for all. In the same way, let your good deeds shine out for all to see, so that everyone will praise your heavenly Father. MATTHEW 5:14-16

Therefore, go and make disciples of all the nations, baptizing them in the name of the Father and the Son and the Holy Spirit. Teach these new disciples to obey all the commands I have given you. And be sure of this: I am with you always, even to the end of the age. MATTHEW 28:19-20

About the Author

Kathleen Long Bostrom loves books—reading them and writing them!

Kathy's first book to be accepted for publication was also the first book in the Questions from Little Hearts series, *What Is God Like?* The poetic questions in that book and this one are based on actual questions from "little hearts" in Kathleen's congregation as well as from her own family. Additional writing credits include another book of verse titled *The World That God Made* and numerous newspaper and magazine articles and several prize-winning sermons.

Kathy has a master of arts degree in Christian education and a master of divinity degree from Princeton Theological Seminary. She also has a bachelor of arts degree in psychology from California State University, Long Beach, California.

Wildwood, Illinois, is where Kathy lives with husband, Greg, and children Christopher, Amy, and David. She and her husband copastor the Wildwood Presbyterian Church.

Kathy hopes that her books will be used not only with parents and children but in Sunday school classes, at preschools, and in church worship settings.

About the Illustrator

Elena Kucharik, well-known Care Bears artist, has illustrated a series for Tyndale House Publishers geared to very young children. These books include *Bible for Little Hearts, Prayers for Little Hearts,* and *Promises for Little Hearts.* For these books, Elena created the Little Blessings characters. As the young readers grow, they—along with their families—can continue to enjoy Elena's Little Blessings characters in this Questions from Little Hearts series.

Born in Cleveland, Ohio, Elena received a bachelor of fine arts degree in commercial art from Kent State University. After graduation she worked as a greeting card artist and art director at American Greetings Corporation in Cleveland, Ohio.

For the past twenty-five years Elena has been a freelance illustrator. During some of that time she was the lead artist and developer of Care Bears as well as a designer and illustrator for major corporations and publishers. For the last seven years Elena has been focusing her talents on illustrations for children's books.

Elena and her husband live in New Canaan, Connecticut, and have two grown daughters.

Books in the *Little Blessings* line

Bible for Little Hearts
Prayers for Little Hearts
Promises for Little Hearts
Lullabies for Little Hearts

What Is God Like?
Who Is Jesus?
What about Heaven?

Blessings Everywhere
Rain or Shine
God Makes Nighttime Too